Apple Watch ECG

The ultimate ECG Interpretation's Guide How to analyze Apple watch ECG like a Professional

Philip Knoll

Intentionally left blank

APPLE WATCH ECG
The Ultimate ECG Interpretation's Guide
How to Analyses Apple watch ECG
like a Professional

76 BPM 10:09

22sec
It helps to rest your arms on a table or your legs.

een Protector

Philip Knoll

ISBN; 9781794246256

**Printed in the United States of America
Graw-Hill Publishing House**

**2 Penn Plaza,
NY 10121
New York
USA**

Dedication

To Philip parents, patty jean, James Knoll and my loving wife Diana, may son Kevin who are a constant source of love, and encouragement .

Checks out my other books .

www.amazon.com/dp/B07FS33G5Y

https://www.amazon.com/dp/B07ML4DXTR

Table of Contents

Introduction

I *want to thank you and congratulate you for downloading the book, "Apple Watch ECG The ultimate ECG Interpretation Guide, How to analyze Apple watch ECG like a Professional". This book contains proven steps and strategies on how to master your Apple watch ECG app perfectly like a professional*

Thanks again for downloading this book, I hope you enjoy it!

The Doctor on Your Wrist

James David thought he was having a panic attack. He took a break from work to walk around the block during a stressful day and noticed he felt out of breath strolling up a slight incline. This isn't normal, James thought. He had become an enthusiastic cycle in recent months and wasn't exactly out of shape.

He sat down at his desk and looked at the Apple Watch series on his wrist.

His heart rate was very high, and the Apple Watch ECG app he was using to check his pulse was flashing warnings. Maybe it was a bit more serious, he thought.

Although he had a pulmonary embolism two years back. He had been on medication, and doctors said that it was an unusual condition for somebody in their mid 20s. Still, the symptoms this time were much less severe, and he was feeling stressed, so his mind didn't automatically jump to blood clots. James's doctor told him it sounded like acute anxiety. Then he showed him a log of his heart rate recorded by the Apple Watch ECG app.

"This is my normal heart rate," James told him, pointing to the graph in the app. "This is where my heart is now. There's something wrong."The doctor ordered for a CT scan. The CT scan result indicates blood clots in his left lung had returned.

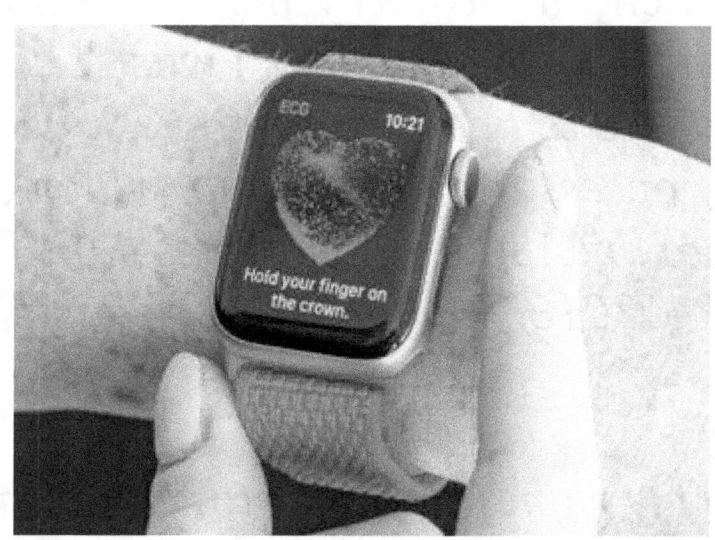

An ambulance rushed James to the emergency room, where he was pumped full of blood thinners. He didn't need surgery this time, but doctors told him that if he had waited, a clot could have killed him. James isn't the only person who has discovered a serious health condition after seeing heart-rate data on an Apple smartwatch. And he won't be the last.

How Apple watches are saving Lives

I was worried when I opened the ECG app for the first time on the Apple Watch Series 4.
I have no known heart issues. I'm a strict discipl inarian about regular physicals. But I had never been to any cardiologist or had an electrocardio gram, and I was a little frightened that the Apple Watch might notify me something about my health that I didn't know. I wasn't confident I even wanted to know. Nevertheless, when I got untimely access to the ECG app, which officially rolls out to my Apple watch series 4 on Thursda y, Dec. 24 2018, I had to make an effort for myself.

I pressed my right forefinger touching the watc h's Digital Crown and held it there for 30 second s as the watch measured my heart rhythm, but t rying not to hold my breath at the same time. I watched my heart beat graphed in real time on the Apple watch screen, trying to interpret on m y own if it was normal. It seemed normal, but I'm no professional about it. The end result displays: Sinus Rhythm. No atrial fibrillation det *ected. I clenched my fist in the air, realizing that I had actually been a little concerned.*

Preferably, you'll never need to use the Apple Watch's ECG app. Except if you feel something strange, a fluttering in your chest or your pulse. You can take what's similar to a clinical single lead electrocardiogram directly on your wrist using Apple watch. This could be the very important lifesaver. Literally, ECG and EKG are both abbreviations for an electrocardiogram, which measures the electrical activity of the heart. Doctors and other health professionals often refer to it as an EKG; Apple's watch app is called it ECG.

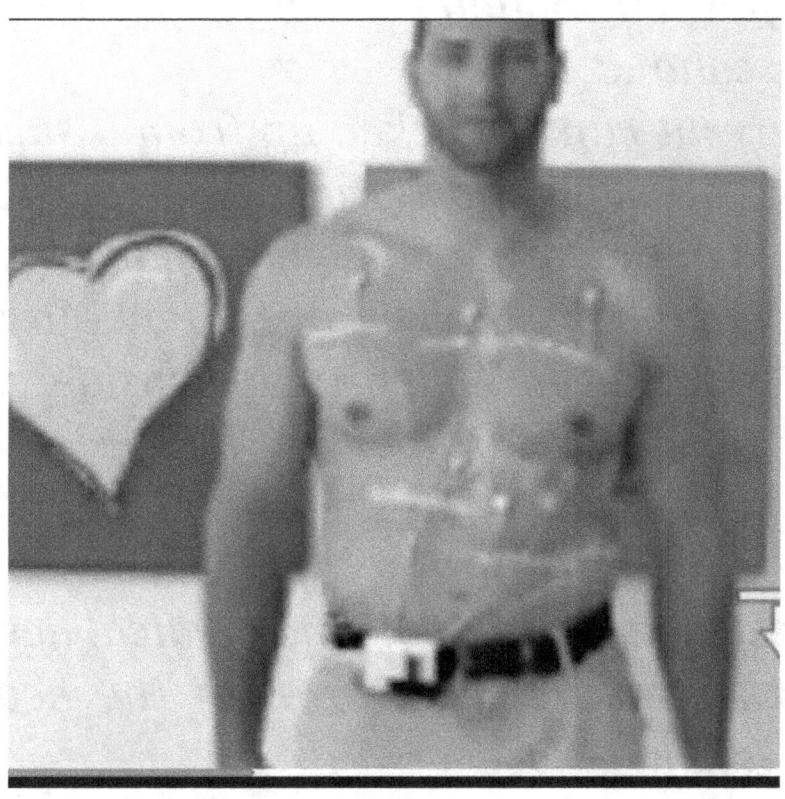

Chapter 1

What you need to know about ECG

E electrocardiography is the scientific procedure by which electrical activities of the heart are analyzed and studied. The spread of excitation through heart muscles myocardium produces a local electrical potential. This low intensity current flows throughout a body, which acts as a volume conductor.

This current can be picked up from a surface of the body by using appropriate electrodes and recorded in the form of an electrocardiogram. The technique initially discovered by Dutch physiologist, Einthoven Willem, who considered as the father of electrocardiogram (ECG).

Electrocardiograph

The electrocardiograph is the medical device by which the electrical activities of the heart are analyzed and recorded.

Electrocardiogram

Electrocardiogram derives from electrocardiogram in Dutch EKG or ECG is the graphical record of electrical activities of the heart, which occur prior to the onset of mechanical activities. It is the sum of electrical activity of cardiac muscle fibers, recorded from the surface of the body.

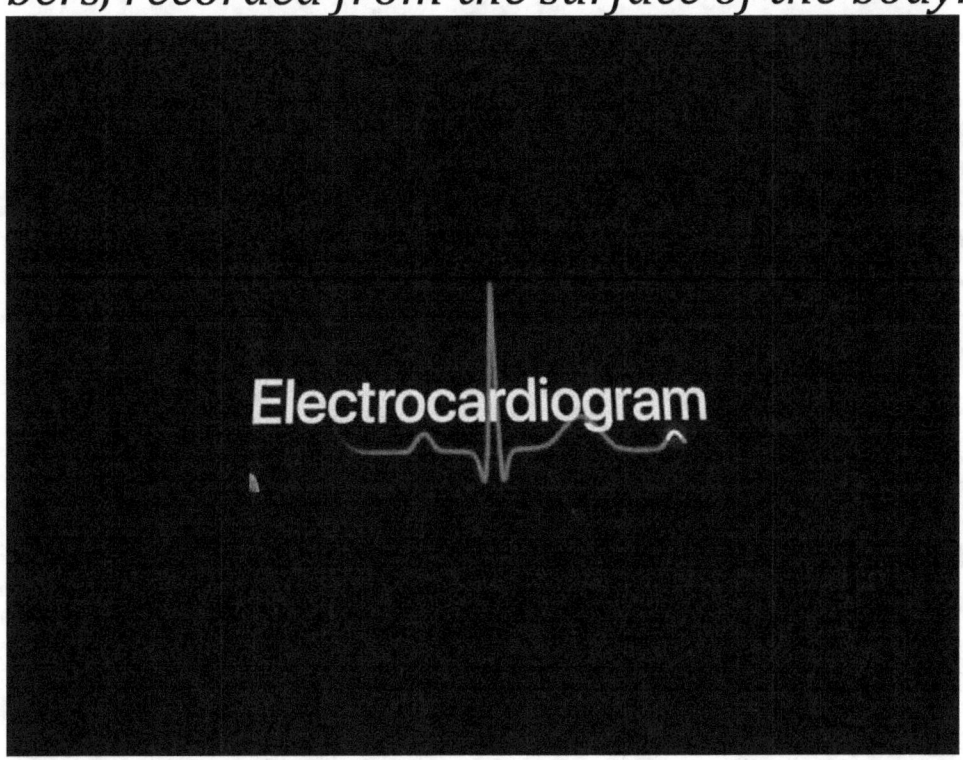

General functions of ECG

The electrocardiogram is very useful in determining and diagnosing the following heart parameters.

1. *Heart rate*
2. *Heart rhythm*
3. *Abnormal electrical conduction*
4. *Poor blood supply to heart muscle (ischemia)*
5. *Heart attack*
6. *Heart coronary artery disease*
7. *Hypertrophy of heart chambers.*

ECG GRID

The paper that is used for recording ECG is called ECG paper.ECG device amplifies the electrical signals produced from the heart and records these signals on a moving ECG paper. Electrocardiographic grid refers to the markings lines on ECG paper. ECG paper has horizontal and vertical lines at regular intervals of 1 mm each. Every 5th line (5mm)is bolded.

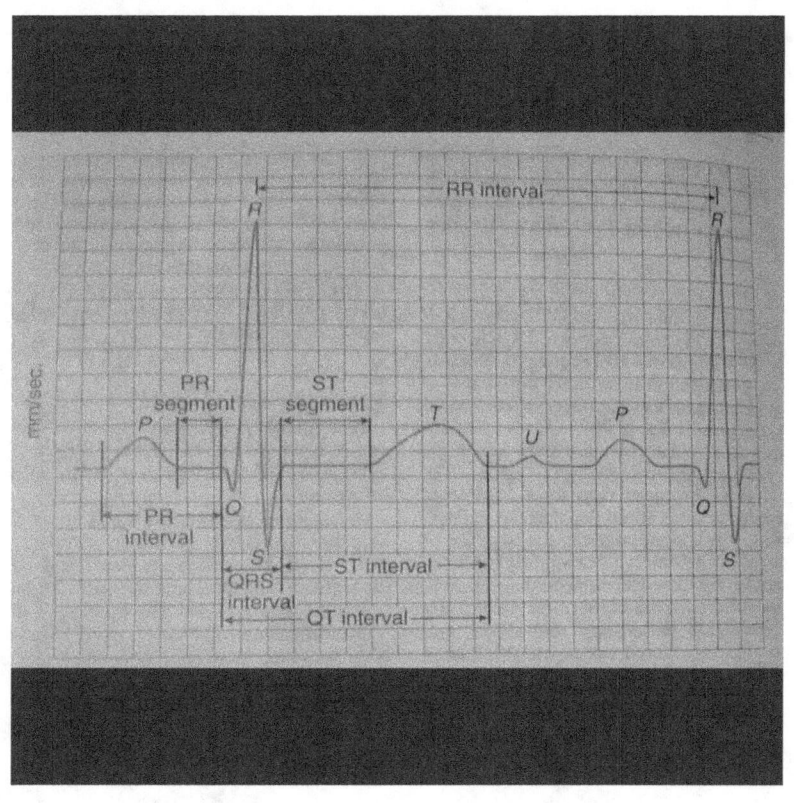

Time duration

The time duration of different ECG waves is usually plotted on horizontally on X-axis.

On X-axis
1 mm = 0.04 second
5 mm = 0.20 second
   Amplitude
An amplitude of ECG waves is plotted vertically on Y-axis.
On Y-axis
1 mm = 0.1 mV
5 mm = 0.5 mV

The speed of the paper

The paper movement through the machine can be adjusted by two speeds, 25 mm/second and 5 0 mm/second. Frequently, a speed of the paper during recording is set at 25 mm/second. If hear t rate is very high, a speed of the paper is chang ed to 50 mm/second.

Chapter 2

How the ECG App Works

*T*he Apple Watch cannot identify heart att acks, high blood pressure, blood clots or any condition aside from atrial fibrillation, which is an irregular heart rhythm that can be, but isn't necessarily, related to those heart issues.*

Is It Accurate?

My watch told me I was in Sinus Rhythm multiple times, and I believed it. But to ensure everything is alright I subjected myself to a 12 le ad electrocardiogram in a hospital, at least, for science. Like the Apple Watch's ECG, a full EKG takes just 30 seconds. The ECG app's results are not comparable to a 12 lead EKG, because the w atch's sensor is similar to a single lead, measuri ng a single point on the body. To be more clear,

Apple does not advocate comparing the two, because they are not the same. A 12-lead EKG can be used to diagnose an array of issues, including heart attacks. A single-lead ECG cannot do that.

My physician attached 12 leads to my body across my chest, arms and legs — to measure the electrical pulses from head to toe. Each lead reveals different information, but it is likely to diagnose atrial fibrillation from a single lead. You can also measure high and low heart rate from one lead, but that's about it.

My full EKG finally confirmed that my heart rhythm is indeed normal no atrial fibrillation detected. Wow. I tried simultaneously undergoing the EKG and taking a measurement in the Apple ECG app, but due to the electrical interference resulted in a noisy reading.

We also learn that last year during world cup, most of the England fans warned about their heart rates during a tense penalty shootout. Apple Watches warned England fans that there could be something seriously wrong with their heart during the team's penalty shootout against Colombia. The stress of watching the game sent pulses rocketing among fans forced to watch *their team fight to stay in the World Cup. Imagine!*

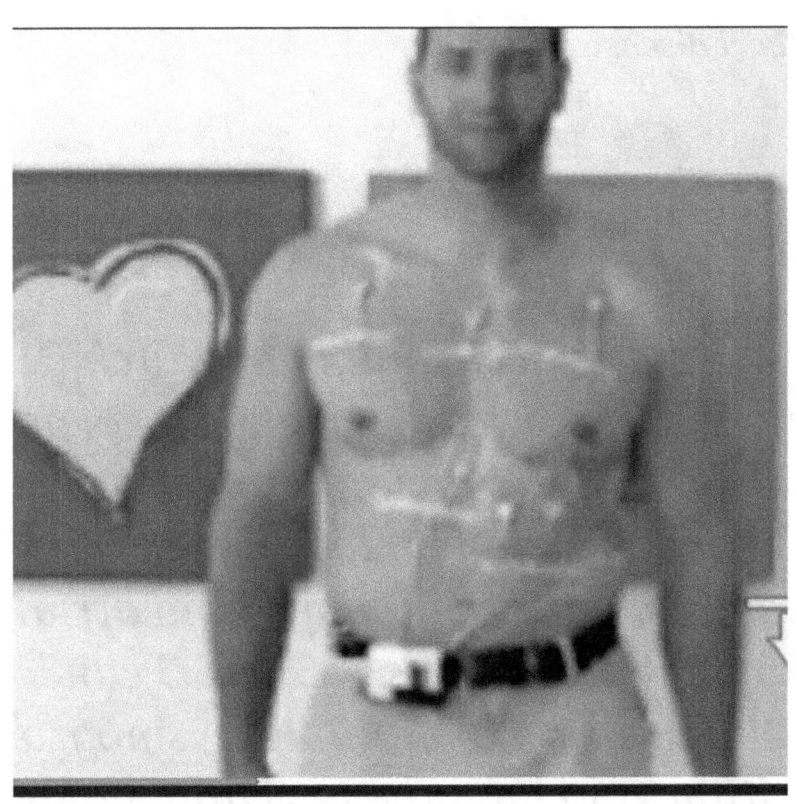

Chapter 3

Apple Watch for heart diseases detection

W ith the accessibility of watch OS 5.1.2 and Apple Watch Series 4, which is incorpo rated with ECG capability, Apple Watch custome rs nowadays have access to two features to dete ct heart problem such as arrhythmias and atrial fibrillation. Apple Watch Series 1, 2 and 3 can l ook for arrhythmias using a photoplethysmogra phbased algorithm, and bu t, the ECG app on Ap ple Watch Series 4 is capable of generating an E CG similar to a Lead I electrocardiogram. This a pp also classifies an ECG as sinus rhythm (SR), a trial fibrillation (AF), or inconclusive, and repor ts high or low heart rate. This book is intended t o provide a more detailed understanding of the capabilities of these features, including testing a nd validation.

The Atrial fibrillation

Atrial fibrillation is a type of irregular heart rhythm in which the upper heart chamber called atria that

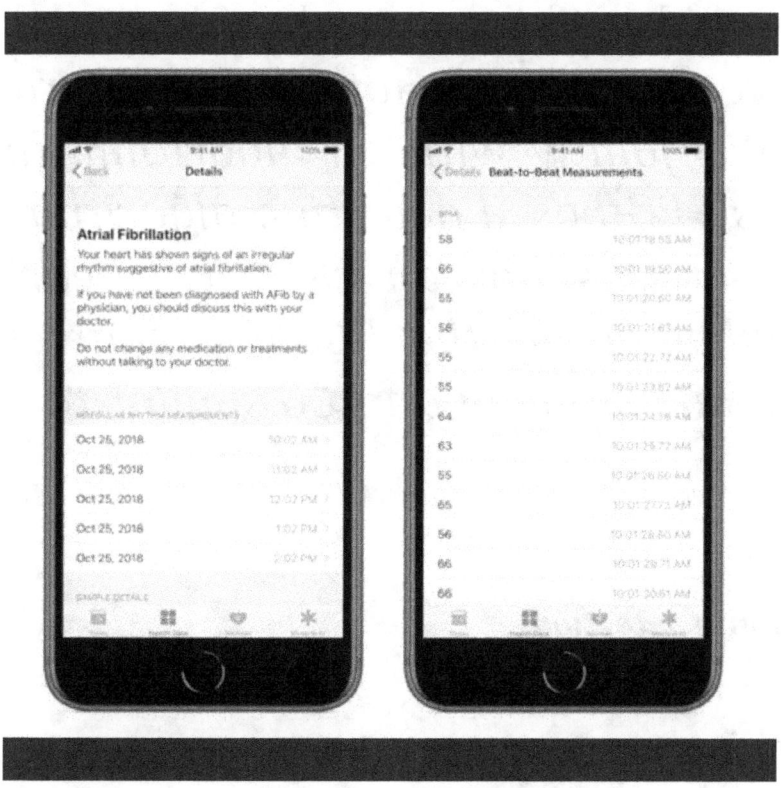

beat irregularly and sometimes rapidly, is a one of the leading cause of stroke. Though, AF is often asymptomatic, leading many persons with AF to be unacquainted with this condition. The mix ture of stroke risk, asymptomatic presentation, effective pharmacologic treatments reducing str oke risk, and increasing market infiltration of co nsumer devices with the potential to discover AF have increased much interest in the early detection of AF outside the clinical setting.

The watchOS 5.1.2, Apple Watch Series 1, 2and 3 are capable of identifying periods of irregular pulse suggestive of AF using photoplethysmogra ph (PPG) signals jointly with an algorithm. In addition to this PPG-based detection algorithm, Apple Watch Series 4 has an electrical heart sensor that, when using the ECG app, enables the generation and study of an ECG similar to a Lead I ECG.

PPG-based arrhythmia detection

Scientific description

Apple Watch has a unique optical heart sensor that uses green LED lights at back surface to paired with light-sensitive photodiodes to detect blood pulses in a user's wrist using Photoplethy smography(PPG). These sensors and essential algorithms are the basis for the heart rate and *heart rate variability (HRV) detection enabled on Apple Watch Series 1 and rest.*

For determination of HRV, Apple Watch captures a tachogram, a plot of the time linking heartbeats, every 2 to 4 hours. Beginning with watch OS 5.1.2, a user may choose to enable an arrhythmia detection aspect that utilizes these tachograms. To use the irregular Rhythm Notifi cation feature on Apple Watch, a user must initial complete onboarding within the Health app on the user's paired iPhone to learn how to use the feature and receive tutoring rega rding AF.

When the PPG-based arrhythmia detection is enabled, each tachogram is classified by means of a proprietary algorithm to determine if an irregular rhythm may be present. An irregular t achogram initiates a surge of more frequent tac hogram collection (as often as possible, subject to a bare minimum spacing of 15 minutes) and analysis. Tachograms are collected and analyze d only if the user remains at rest enough to obta in another reading; because of this, the algorith m is not constantly monitoring the user, but to a certain extent is doing so opportunistically whe n an adequate signal is available for collection/analysis. If 5 out of 6 sequential 3 tachograms (including the initial one) are classified as irregular within a 48 hour period of time, the user is notified of the possible arrhythmia. In addition to the arrhythmia notification, the user can also access more information related to these irregular tachograms within the Health app

If two tachograms are classified as not irregular prior to the threshold is reached, the cycle is automatically reset and tachogram collection returns to the baseline rate (every 2 hours).

Preclinical development test

preceding to clinical testing, numerous studies were conducted to build up the PPG based detection algorithm and to evaluate algorithm performance across a diversity of environmental conditions and user behaviors. Among these were normal sleeping, deep breathing, riding in a car, hand tremors and motion, reduced hand and wrist perfusion, overnight wear rapid ventricular response in those with AF and other arrhythmias. These studies were performed in 2500 control subjects and more than 600 subjects with AF.

Because PPG relies on LED light absorptivity, the arrhythmia detection algorithm was tested across different types of skin and tones to ensure that sense platform adjustments for skin tone were adequate in the framework of the algorithms used to detect arrhythmias. The skin contains Melanin that has high absorptivity at the wavelength used by the green LED on the Apple smartwatch, making PPG heart rate measurement potentially more complex in darker skin tones. To rectify this, the Apple Watch sensing platform adjusts LED current and thus light output, photodiode gain (sensitivity to emitted light), and sampling rate to ensure adequate signal amplitude across all the variety of human skin tone.

In the Apple watch Health app, users can see the times when the algorithm identified an irregular tachogram that contributed to a notification on the (left).
Selecting one of these specific dates or times allows a user to visualize the beat-to-beat measurements calculated from both tachogram.

Health App View of Irregular Rhythm Measurements

For validation purposes, 1.4 million tachograms from 1134 subjects (52% female) with varying skin type and tone (Fitzpa trick skin type and sp ectrophotometer measured skin lightness at the wrist) were studied and analyzed.

In fact, the primary manufacturing concerns foc used on signal amplitudes in persons with dark skin, nearly 5% of enrolled subjects had Fitzpatr ick type VI skin, about twice the expected preval ence in the United states population.

 The Validation efforts confirmed no significant difference in algorithm sensitivity or specificity across skin types/tones.

Clinical Validation from Apple Heart Study

The Apple Heart Study centre(AHS) is a forthco ming, single arm pragmatic study conducted vir tually to evaluate the ability of the Apple Watch base irregular pulse notification algorithm to id entify arrhythmia suggestive of AF. Contained by AHS, if a user met the requirement of 5/6 irre gular tachogram threshold, the user received an Apple Watch and *iPhone notification and had the option of contacting a telehealth physician and being sent an ambulatory ECG patch. Participants instructed to wear the ePatch for up to one week; however, data collected from a participant were considered adequate with a minimum analyzable time of two hours.*

Chapter 5

Apple watch ECG Description

Apple Watch Series 4 comes to a titanium electrode in their digital crown and an ultra thin chromium silicon carbon nitride layer applied to the sapphire crystal on the back of the Apple Watch. The ECG app detects and records the electrical impulses that control the heart from the user's fingertip on a digit

al crown and the wrist on back of the Apple Watch, which creates a short closed circuit. for using the ECG app on Apple Watch, a user must initially complete onboarding within the Health and fitness app on the user's paired iPhone to learn more on how to use the element and receive instruction regarding AF. To make an ECG, a user must open the ECG app installed on Apple Watch, then apply a finger from the hand contralateral to the wrist of the hand where Apple Watch is worn to the digital crown for 30 seconds. Lead I polarity is determined by the wrist placement of Apple Watch that already selected in Settings.

Subsequent to obtaining the ECG, an algorithm is used to classify the ECG tracing as Sinus Rhythms (SR), atrial fibrillation (AF), or inconclusive. This rhythms classification, on average heart rate, user reported symptoms, and waveform are all stored in HealthKit and can be sent by the user as a PDF file from the Health app on the user's paired iPhone to the physicians.

ECG determination on Apple Watch

The Apple Watch was publicly the remarkable events on September 9, 2014, in Cupertino at the Flint Center. It is the renowned symbolic place where Steve Jobs introduced the first Macintosh in 1984 and iMac in 1998 respectively.

After presenting a sequence of their new products and services, the current Apple CEO Tim Cook abruptly came back on stage with the memorable Steve Job's signature and he says "One more thing…".

It was the first tributes the death of Jobs, a sign that the company was at last willing to let the Jo bs legacy lie. He then introduced the most perso nal device Apple has ever created in the history of humankind.

Apple initial released in April 2015 its new line of product in three collections: Apple Watch, Ap ple Watch Sport, and Apple Watch Edition. The company described the products on as follows: The (Apple watch...) collection features highly p olished stainless steel and space black stainless s teel cases. The face display is protected by sapph ire crystal. And there's a choice of three special l eather bands, a link bracelet, a Milanese loop, a nd a band made from the high-performance fluoro-elastomer component.

Conditions of functionality

The brand of Apple watch runs a version of iOS, different from its smart phone counterpart, but is not making calls from the watch without bein g connected to a compatible Apple smart watch. But other important functions are availa ble such as notifications, activity, Siri, Apple Pay etc.

ECG App Instructions guide

Indications for use

The ECG app is an Apple watch software for only mobile medical application intended for use with the Apple Watch series to create, record, store, transfer, and display a single channel electrocardiogram (ECG) similar to a Lead I ECG of the standard lead I, II, and III.

The ECG app can determine the incidence of atrial fibrillation (AF) or sinus rhythm on a classifiable waveform. But the Apple watch ECG app is not suggested for users with other known typical arrhythmias.

The ECG app is basically intended for over-the-counter (OTC) use only. The data displayed by the Apple watch ECG app is intended for information only. The user is not intended to interpret or take any clinical action based on the Apple watch ap output without consultation of a qualified healthcare professional.

The ECG waveform is intended to supplement rhythm classification for the purposes of discrimin ating AF from typical normal sinus rhythm and not intended to replace conventional methods of diagnosis or treatment. The Apple ECG app is also not applicable to people under age of 22.

Chapter 6

Using the ECG App

App Set-Up/On-boarding
The ECG app is available on Apple Watch Series 4 with watchOS 5.1.2 or later generation, paired with iPhone 5s or later with iOS 12.1.1.

•Open the Health app on your iPhone.
•In the Health Data tab, tap Heart, then select "Electrocardiogram (ECG)"
•Follow the screen instructions.
•You may exit on-boarding at any time by pressing "Cancel."

Recording an Apple ECG

•Ensure your Apple Watch is snug on the wrist you selected in Settings > General > Watch Orientation.

•*Open the ECG app on your Apple smart Watch.*
•*Rest your arms on your lap or in the table, and hold your finger on the Digital Crown. No need t o press the crown during the session.*
•*The recording takes almost 30 seconds.*

Apple watch ECG Analysis

•*After a successful reading, you will receive one of the following classifications notifications on your ECG app:*
1. Sinus Rhythm: A normal sinus rhythm result means the heart is beating in a uniform pattern between 50-100 BPM.

2. Atrial Fibrillation: An AF result means the heart is beating in an irregular pattern between 50-120 BPM.

3.Inconclusive: An inconclusive result means that the recording can't be well classified. This can occur for many reasons such as not resting your arms on a table during a recording, or your Apple Watch is too loosen your wrist. Some physiological conditions may prevent a small percentage of Apple users from creating enough signals to produce a good recor ding result.

4. Low or High Heart Rate: A heart rate under 50 BPM (beat per minute) or over 120 BPM affe cts the ECG app's capability to check for AF and the recording is considered inconclusive.

After an Apple watch ECG recording is complete, the ECG data is analyzed to establish if it is at least 25 seconds long, and, if so, if either Sinus Rhythm or AF is present, or if an Inconclusive result is acceptable.

The ECG recording result on the ECG app provides a detailed display of the result. A comp rehensive explanation will also be provided on your iPhone.

Presence of AF in your ECG results may represent only potential findings. If you are experiencing any symptoms, contact your physic ian. If you believe you are experiencing any sort of medical emergency, you should contact emergency services.

When it displays a result of Sinus Rhythm it means that your heart rate is between 50 and 100 beats per minute and is beating in a unifor m pattern and within normal ranges.

But when it displays inconclusive ECG results may mean that there may have been too much artifact or noise to acquire a high-quality signal, or you may have an arrhythmia other than AF the app cannot classify, or your heart rate is between 100 and 120 BPM.

A small percentage of people may have definite physiological conditions preventing the user from getting enough signal to produce a good result.

You may learn more about Inconclusive ECG results during on-boarding, by accessing more information in the ECG area of the Health app on your iPhone, or by tapping the "i" icon on the Apple ECG app for further information.

A heart rate under normal circumstance may be low because of certain medications or if electric al signals are not properly conducted through t he heart muscle. Exercise training to be an athlete can also lead to a low heart rate.

A heart rate may be high because of exercise, stress, nervousness, alcohol dehydration, infection, AF, or other arrhythmias.

If you receive an Inconclusive notifications result due to a poor recording, you might try to re-record your ECG. You can also review how to take an ECG during on boarding or by tapping on

"Take a Recording" in the ECG area of the Health app on the iPhone.

All ECGs are synced to the Health app on your iP hone. You can use the Health app to share your ECG with a clinician.

Safety and performance of Apple watch ECG

The Apple ECG app's ability to accurately classify an ECG recording into AF and normal sinus rhythm were extensively tested in a clinica l trial of approximately 600 subjects.

Rhythm classification of a 12 standard lead ECG by a cardiologist was compared to the rhythm cl assification of a concurrently collected ECG fro m the Apple ECG app. The Apple ECG app establi shed 98.3% sensitivity in classifying AF and 99.6% specificity in classifying sinus rhythm in classifiable recordings.

In this clinical trial, about 12.2% of recordings were inconclusive and not classifiable as either normal sinus rhythm or AF. When inconclusive recordings were included in the analysis, the Apple ECG app *correctly classified sinus rhythm in 90.5% of sub jects with sinus rhythm and AF in 85.2% of subjects with AF. The clinical data validation results reflect use in a controlled environment. Real world use of the Apple ECG app can result in a greater number of strips being deemed inco nclusive and not classifiable.*

The morphology of the waveform was tested in this clinical trial by visual assessment of the standard PQRST wave and R wave amplitude in comparison to a reference. There was a tremend ous success during this clinical trial, no adverse events were observed.

Chapter 7

Apple watch ECG troubleshooting

I   *F you have trouble in operating your Apple ECG app, below are some of the possible p roblems and their solutions.*

1. Problem: I cannot get the ECG app to take my reading.

   Solution :

   • make sure that you have completed all of the on-boarding steps in the Health app on your iPhone.

   • Ensure your wrist and your Apple Watch are clean and dry. Water and sweat may cause a poor recording.

   • make sure that your Apple Watch, arms, and hands remain fixed during recordings.

2. Problem: I have a lot of artifact, noise, or interference in the recording.

Solution:
• Rest your arms on your lap or on the table while you take a recording. Endeavor to rel ax and not move too much.
• Ensure your Apple Watch isn't loose on your wrist. The band should be tightly snug and the back of your Apple Watch needs be touching your wrist.
• Move away from all electronics that are plugged into an outlet to avoid electrical interference.

3. Problem: The ECG waveforms appear upside down instead of upright.

Solution:
• The watch orientation may probability set to the wrong wrist. On your iPhone, go to th e Watch app. Tap My Watch>General> Wat ch Orientation.

All data recorded during an Apple ECG app session is saved to Health app on your iPhone. If you like, you can share that Information by creating a PDF.

You should take note that new ECG data cannot be recorded once your Apple Watch's storage is full. If you are not able to take a recording due to storage space issues, you should free up some space by deleting unwanted apps, music. You can check your storage usage capacity by navigating to the Apple Watch app on your iPhone, tapping "My Watch", tapping "General", and then tapping "Usage".

Precautions

The Apple ECG app cannot check for signs of an impending heart attack. If you believe you're having a medical emergency, call emergency services.

Do not take recordings when Apple Watch is in close neighborhood to strong electromagnetic fields (e.g. electromagnetic anti-theft systems, metal detectors).

Do not take recordings during a medical procedures, such as magnetic resonance imaging, diathermy, lithotripsy, cautery, and external defibrillation.

Do not take recordings when Apple Watch is outside of theoperational optimum temperature range (0 °C – 35°C) and humidity of 20 % to 95% relative humidity.

as indicated in the same author book Apple Watch (Series 4, 2019 Edition)The ultimate user guide, How to master Apple Watch in 2 Hours.

Don't of Apple watch ECG

Do not use it to diagnose heart-related conditions.

Do not use it with a cardiac pacemaker, ICDs, or other implanted electronic devices.

Do not take a recording during active physical activity.

Do not change your medication without consulting your doctor.

You should talk to your physicians if your heart rate is below 50 or over 120 when at rest and because this is an unexpected result.

You should also take note that interpretations made by this Apple watch app are potential findings, not a complete diagnosis of cardiac conditions. The user is not intended take clinical action based on the app outpour without consul tation of a qualified healthcare professional.

The waveform generated by the Apple ECG app is only meant to supplement rhythm classificati on for the purposes of discriminating AF from n ormal sinus rhythm and not intended to replace conventional methods of diagnosis or treatment.

Apple does not fully guarantee that you are not experiencing an arrhythmia or other health con ditions when the Apple ECG app labels an ECG as Sinus Rhythm. You should rather notify your physician if you detect possible changes in your health.

Security tips

Apple recommends that you should add a passc ode (personal identification number [PIN]),

Face ID or Touch ID (fingerprint) to your iPhone and a passcode (personal identification number [PIN]) to your Apple Watch to add more layer of security. It is important to secure your iPhone since you will be storing personal health information.

Chapter 8

Standard ECG components

*T*he standard ECG provides 12 different vectors that view the heart electrics activity. By convention, the ECG tracing is divided into P wave,
PR interval. QRS complex, QT interval, ST segment, T wave and U wave.We are going to discuss the component very briefly here.

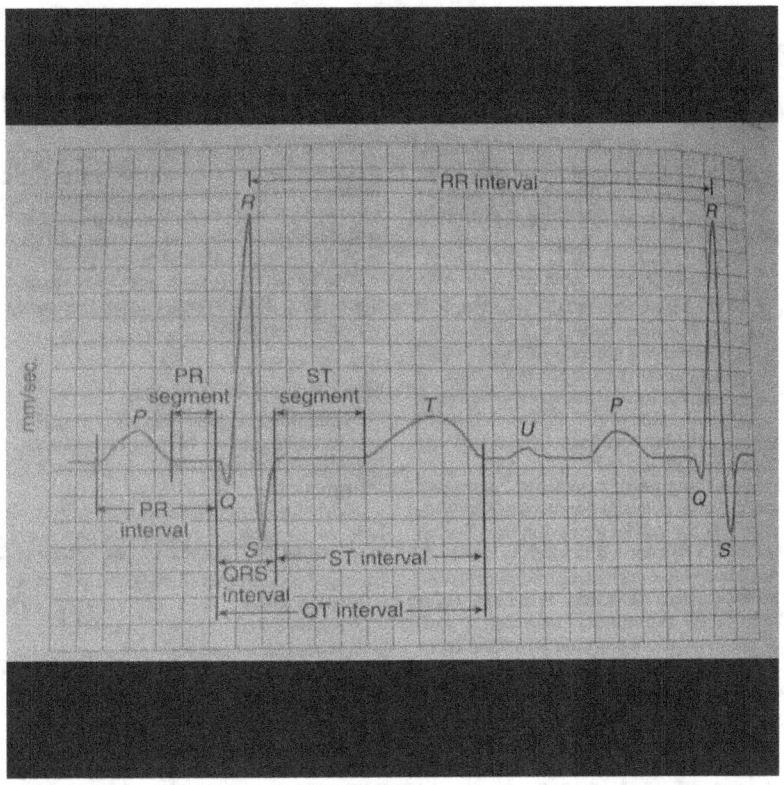

P wave represents atrial depolarization. It is up right in most leads except AvR. It may be bi phas ic in lead II and Vi. The initial component repres ent right atrial activity and 2 nd component represent left atrial activity. An increase in ampl itude of either or both components occur with atrial enlargement. Right atrial enlargement produce a P wave> 2mm in lead II, III and aVf (p pulmonale). Left atrial enlargerment produce a P wave that is broad and double peaked in lead II (P mitrale). Normally, the P axis is between 0^0 and 75^0

The PR interval is the time between onset of atrial depolarization and onset of ventricular de polarization. Normally it is 0.10 to 0.20 sec. prolongation defines 1 [st] degree atrioventricular block.

The QRS complex represents ventricular depolar ization. The Q wave is initial downward deflecti on. Normal Q wave last <0.05 sec in all lead except in Vi-3 I which the Q wave is considered abnormal, indicating part or current infarction; the R wave is the 1st upward deflection; citeria for normal height or size are not absolute, but the taller R may be caused by ventricular hypert rophy. A 2nd upward deflection in a QRS complex is designed R^1 . The S wave is the 2nd downward deflection. Normally, QRS interval is 0.07 to 0.10 sec

The QT interval is the time between onset of ven tricular depolarization and end of ventricular re polarization, the QT interval must correlate wit h heart rate.

The ST segment represents completed ventricular myocardial depolarization. Normally, it is horizontal along the base line of the PR (TP) interval or slightly off base line.

The T wave reflects ventricular repolarization. It is usually take the same direction as the QRS complex.

The U wave appears uncommonly in parsons who have hypokalemia, hypomagnesemia or ischemia.

Interpretation of Abnormal ECG component

1. P wave is abnormal
   The possible causes are left or right hypertrophy, atrial escapes or ectopic beat.

2. P wave absent
   The possible causes are atrial fibrillation, sinus node exit block, hyperkalemia

3. P-P varying
   Possibly due to a sinus arrhythmia

4. PR interval long

Possible causes are first degree atrioventricular block,Mobitz type 1 atrioventricular block or multifocal atrial tachycardia

5. *QRS complex wide*

Possible causes are right or left bundle branch block, ventricular flutter, fibrillation or hyperkalemia

6. *QT interval short*

Possible causes are hyperkalemia, Hyperma gnesemia. Grave's diseases, and digixin drug

7. *ST segment elevation*

Possible causes are myocardial ischemia; acute myocardiac infarction, left bundle branch block, acute pericarditis, left ventricular hypertrophy, hyperkalemia, pulmonary embolism, digoxin drug, normal variation especially in athletics heart syndrome.

8. *ST segment depression*

Possible causes are myocardial ischemia. Acute posterior myocardiac infarction, digoxin drug; ventricular hypertrophy; pulmonary embolism; left bundle branch block; and right bundle block.

9. *T wave tall*
   Possible causes are hyperkalemia, acute myocardiac infarction, left bundle branch block, stroke, and ventricular hypertrophy.

10. *T wave small, flattened or inverted*
    Possible causes are myocardiac ischemia, age, race, hyperventilation, anxiety, drinking hot or cold beverages, left ventricular hypertrophy,certain drugs e.g degoxin, pericarditis, pulmonary embolism, conduction disturbance and electrolyte disturbances.

11. *U wave prominent*
    Possible causes are hypokalemia, hypomanesemia and ischemia.

Conclusion

*Thank you again for downloading this book!
I hope this book was able to help you to use your Apple watch ECG app perfectly and make use of it like a professional.
The next step is to enjoy your watch ECG app.
Finally, if you enjoyed this book, please take the time to share your thoughts and post a review on Amazon. I will be greatly appreciated!
Thank you and good luck*

Check Out My Other Books

Preview Of '*Apple Watch description page.*
'*(Series 4, 2019 Edition)*
The ultimate user guide, How to master Apple Watch in 2 Hours.
Do you have an Apple Watch? They're amazing popular, and an option to just having your phone on your wrist all the time. For those of us that are into Apple products, an Apple Watch might seem like the perfect thing for those who are looking to create a more personalized, and a better manner to take calls and other information.
Well, it is because you have spent a lot of money to purchase the smart Watch, why should not you optimize it. *.Everything changed with the Series 4. It easily stole the show from the iPhone XS and iPhone X'S Max during Apple's fall media event. After spending some time with the Series 4, things have started to become clear. The Apple Watch has graduated from the iPhone's sidekick to a hero all of its own*

The truth is, there is a lot of secret that can optimize your Apple smart Watch Experience. And how to do it, it quite easy and simple. But, how do you use it? What's the best way to get the most out of this? How do you use this watch? Well, you're about to find out. Everything that you need to know about the Apple smart Watch is included in this; along with simplified tips and tricks to better help you understand how to use this. By the end of this, you'll know exactly how to use the Apple Watch.

Here is a preview of what you'll learn:

- *The releases of series 4*
- *10 coolest things about Apple the Watch*
- *Detail review of Apple Watch series 4*
- *Things you didn't know about Apple Watch*
- *Best Apple Watch Application*
- *Best Apple Watch games*
- *General quick with the watch face*
- *How to optimize it*
- *Basic configuration*
- ***Safety, Handling, of Apple Watch***
- *What each single icon means on this watch*
- *How to add friends on the Apple Watch*

- *How to monitor your workouts and heart rate*
- *Top Apple smart Watch gadget you must have*
- *Wonderful tips and tricks, along with simplified information and new things that you can do with the Apple watch to get the most out of this.*
- *And much more..!*

With the Apple Watch, it might seem like a newer system that you don't understand how to use. That's fine, it's totally okay. But, with this book, you'll be able to learn everything that you need to know about the Apple Watch, and how to better master it. You'll be able to use this watch in a successful way and know how to not just do all of the basic functions, but also how to master other cool tips and tricks as well. With new generations of this coming out, it's worth learning more about, so that you can use this su ccessfully.

***Get** your copy of "Apple Watch"*

https://www.amazon.com/dp/B07ML4DXTR

Preview of APPLE WATCH
2018 Apple watch user Guide including tips and tricks.

Introduction

This might not be in the main area of being cool but it was appealing marvelous. Last week I went out to start my generator and I gave it a big ole pull and accidentally off flies my Apple Watch Series 3 from my wrist, it flew through the air about 20 yards and fell into my thousand liters water tank which was actually the lid off. Nevertheless, there is my five-month old Apple watch in the bottom of a thousand liters of water. But Mind you my tank is about four feet tall and about six feet wide with an opening of about 15 inches, my first contemplation was, "waterproofing tech don't fail." After about 25 minutes of fishing around with a bait of magnet, I pulled my Apple Watch out of its soggy resting lair and it was just fine and working perfectly.

Why do you need Apple Watch?
There are so many reasons for using Apple Watc h because it comes with different amazing funct ionality. When using the Apple Watch, it can monitor your heart rate and mind you your heart rate is the most essential among the vital sign of your life. The Apple Watch uses photople thysmography technology (PPG) which uses the green LED lights to measure your heart rates. To determine a user's heart rate, the Apple watch flashes green light from the LEDs at the skin of user's and detects the amount of this light that is absorbed by the red pigment of your blood. The following are some of the reasons why you need an Apple Watch.

Why should we use Apple watch?
1.   Easy access to your phone information   and including all your notifications
2. Your watch can easily respond to the text quickly and phone calls can be simply taken from your wrist with the feeling of satisfaction
3. The Apple watch has an excellent fitness track er/companion and that can be used for all your workout needs and exercise

4. The watch also came with preinstalled applic ations that are well designed and functional

5. The new Series 2 and 3 is absolutely waterpro of so you can wear the watch almost everywher e

6. It has good battery life much better it was advertised

Generation of Apple watches

Generally speaking, Apple Watch was initially released in April 2015 as the first generation Apple Watch, As of October 2017, three generations, a nd four series of Apple Watch have been release d. The series in bold are currently produced:

1.   Apple Watch from 2015 to 2016

2.   Apple Watch Series 1 from 2016 to present

3.   Apple Watch Series 2 from 2016 to 2017

4.   Apple Watch Series 3 from 2017–present

5. Apple watch series 4 from 2018- date

The Apple Watch Series 2 and Series 3 models are further divided into four "Apple Watch collection":

* *Apple Watch,*
* *Apple Watch Nike+*

- *Apple Watch Hemes*
- *Apple Watch Edition.*

The only differences between these Apple smart Watch collections are differentiated solely by co mbinations of their cases, bands, and exclusive watch faces. The first collection Apple Watch comes with either aluminium or stainless steel c ases or different watch bands; the second collect ion Apple Watch Nike+ utilizes aluminium cases and special types of sport band; the third collection of Apple Watch Hemes comes with stainless steel cases and Hemes watch bands; w hile the fourth collection of Apple smartWatch Edition comes with ceramic versions cases.

But for the Apple Watch Series 1 models they only come with aluminum cases and sports bands. And finally, Apple smartWatch Series 3 models are sold with a modification that allows for cellular LTE capability.
All models come in either 38- or 42-millimeter body, with the 42 mm size having a little larger screen and battery. However, all Apple Watch models have various color and band style.
Apple made bands consist of colored sports ban ds, sports loop, woven nylon band, classic

buckle, modern buckle, leather loop, Milanese loop, and a link bracelet.

The latest series of Apple Watch

It's one of the most frequent questions among people looking to get the Apple Watch for the first time – what does this smartwatch really do? Have you wondered why many want to get the latest series of the Apple watch? Do you want to learn the best ways to utilize your watch and maximize its efficiency?

You are on the right path to learning the most effective ways to utilize your Apple Watch using this book.

Obviously, your watch has a lot more than just a mere chance to read text messages and answer calls on your wrist, to a certain extent than your phone, which is the main common characteristic everyone knows.

The Apple Watch is a capable fitness tracker, with some world-class features, and can double as a sports watch, as well. Yes, you can use less time looking at your phone with wrist notifications funct on, and thanks for having Siri function on your wrist, setting alarms, timers, and reminders are straightforward, too. Subsequently, there are dedicated applications. Starting from board ing passes to traffic notifications and even your walking directions, wow! This it's an incredibly personal experience from your Apple Watch. The recent launch of watch OS 4 as well, refreshed the features on that put forward. For instance, including a sophisticated heart rate metrics, new watch faces, and an alarm that can inform you about your heart status and it can even tell you what is going wrong, and these wonderful features are set to become widesprea d in use today.

The Apple Watch has an indisputably sharp learning curve, and the first days can be a little annoying for the amateur. This composes of all the new features and edge tweaks from watch and ones coming from series 3 and 4.

More ever, If there is one major difference between the Apple Watch and the competitors it 's the wideness of apps. Apple Watch is Just like the iPhone, Apple has missed the killer features of the Apple Watch up to its army of developers. The Apple Watch is an extremely good fitness tr acker and can also track your workouts. Howev er, if you have a Series 2 or Series 3 with GPS fun ctions, it can substitute your ordinary fitness wa tch. Others popular applications such as keeps t abs on movement apps, calories burned app and standing time, which can be encouraged you to 'close the rings' in order to make your daily goals.

But for the Workout app is a special beast, and allows you to track a group of different activitie s, from running and cycling to indoor workouts. These will essentially just keep tabs on your hea rt rate, amount of calories and time spent.

www.amazon.com/dp/B07FS33G5Y

NOTE

About the Author

Philip Knoll is CEO of McGraw publishing compan y that published several IT books. He worked at Interoute, Europe's largest voice and data netw ork provider. Before Interoute, he was working as a senior network engineer for Globtel Interne t, a significant Internet and Telephony Services Provider to the market. He has been working with Linux for more than 10 years putting a strong accent on security for protecting vital data from hackers and ensuring good quality se rvices for internet customers. Moving to VoIP services he had to focus even more on security as sensitive billing data is most often stored on servers with public IP addresses. He has been studying QoS implementations on Linux to build different types of services for IP customers and also to deliver good quality for them and for VoIP over the public Internet. Philip has also bee n programming educational software's with Per l, PHP, and Smarty for over 7 years mostly devel oping in-house management interfaces for IP and VoIP services.